GUIDED BY HIS LIGHT
Christmas Lessons For Every Season

John Stanko

Guided By His Light
by John W. Stanko
Copyright ©2025 John W. Stanko

ISBN 978-1-63360-334-9

All rights reserved. This book is protected under the copyright laws of the United States of America. This book may not be copied or reprinted for com-mercial gain or profit.

Scripture quotations are taken from THE HOLY BIBLE: New International Version ©1978 by the New York International Bible Society, used by permission of Zondervan Bible Publishers. All rights reserved.

For Worldwide Distribution   Printed in the USA

Urban Press
PO Box 5044
Williamsburg, VA 23188
757.808.5776
www.urbanpress.us

Introduction

I wrote *Guided By His Light* to help you recognize and trust God's direction in every season of life. To be honest, I really didn't write it—I compiled it. It is a gathering of my material that I've written over many years, both in books and online. While the readings follow the Advent and Christmas calendar, from late November through the end of December, the truths within are timeless and applicable any time of year. Whenever you find yourself uncertain about your next step, you can return to this devotional to be reminded that God still speaks, leads, and provides. In short, He is a great communicator.

That is why I have taught over the years that guidance should not be a problem for those who follow Christ. If you are "following" Him, that means He is going somewhere. If He wants you to follow, which of course He does, then He must make the way clear. You have to be able to see or hear Him to follow His direction. I've always relied on John 7:17 when it comes to guidance: "Anyone who wants to do the will of God *will know* whether my teaching is from God or is merely my own" (NLT, emphasis added). If you commit to do God's will *before* you know what it is, then you will have no problem knowing what it is. It may take time, but it will become clear. That is my experience and testimony, and I think Scripture backs me up.

Each day's entry includes a Scripture verse, a brief reflection that ties biblical truth to everyday life, and two reflection questions to help you personalize what you've read. Almost every devotional draws from my own experiences—stories of ministry, travel, writing, and learning to follow God's voice one step at a time. I 've never been very good at including third-party testimonies in my teaching. God has always had me use my own life examples.

My prayer is that as you work through these pages, you'll not only celebrate the birth of Christ but also rediscover the joy of walking closely with Him. May you see that divine guidance isn't limited to angels, dreams, or stars—it comes through obedience, faith, and daily trust. Whether you're ending a difficult season, beginning a new year, making a major decision, or simply seeking reassurance that God is with you, may this devotional remind you that His light will always lead you home.

Dr. John Stanko
Williamsburg, VA
November 2025

Listening for Direction

"Your word is a lamp for my feet,
a light on my path."
– Psalm 119:105

Many people want God to reveal the whole map before they take the first step of the journey. Yet Scripture tells us that His Word is not a floodlight revealing miles ahead, but a lamp giving just enough light for the next few steps. Walking in divine guidance requires trust, not total understanding.

When God first stirred my heart to start PurposeQuest International, I didn't have a business plan, staff, or even a clear funding model. All I had was a burden to help people discover their purpose and a conviction that I must begin. I remember sitting in prayer one day and realizing that if I waited until everything was clear, I would never start. So I moved ahead with the little light I had—and God has met me every step of the way. Partners came. Opportunities appeared. The lamp illuminated the next patch of path only as I moved forward.

That's the rhythm and pattern of God's guidance: revelation follows obedience. You take one step in faith, and the next becomes visible. Advent reminds us that Jesus Himself was the Light of the World who entered our darkness one step at a time—first a promise, then a manger, then a cross.

Reflection Questions

Where are you hesitating because you can't see the entire road ahead?

What step of obedience could you take today, trusting that God will illuminate the next?

Day 2

Mary's Yes

"'I am the Lord's servant,' Mary answered. 'May your word to me be fulfilled.'" – Luke 1:38

Mary didn't receive a clear roadmap—only a revelation. When Gabriel announced that she would bear the Son of God, she could not foresee the gossip, the travel, or the pain that awaited her. Yet she believed God would guide her through obedience.

Guidance often begins with surrender before clarity. We want understanding before obedience, but God usually asks for obedience before understanding. Mary's "yes" became the turning point of history because she trusted the character of the One giving the instruction more than she feared the cost of obedience.

You may be facing a call that stretches your comfort or upends your expectations. Remember Mary's example: God's favor doesn't guarantee ease—it guarantees His presence. Advent invites you to echo her faith-filled words: "May it be to me as You have said."

Reflection Questions

What situation requires you to say 'yes' to God before you know the outcome?

How can Mary's example of trust help you respond with surrender rather than fear?

Day 3

Joseph's Dream

"When Joseph woke up, he did what the angel of the Lord had commanded him and took Mary home as his wife." – Matthew 1:24

Joseph's guidance came while he slept. When logic concerning his situation offered only disappointment,

God spoke through a dream. Divine direction often reaches us in the quiet spaces where we finally stop analyzing and start listening.

Joseph's obedience was immediate. He didn't hold a family meeting or request more proof; he simply did what the angel said. The road of faith is rarely comfortable—it demands courage to act when clarity is partial. Joseph's decision protected Mary, preserved the Messiah's lineage, and fulfilled prophecy.

God may be speaking to you through Scripture, counsel, or a whisper in the night. The key is readiness. When Joseph woke up, he didn't wait until the timing made sense—he obeyed. Perhaps your next breakthrough will come after you "wake up" and act on what God already told you.

Reflection Questions

Has God ever guided you through an unexpected source or quiet prompting?

What step of obedience have you delayed while waiting for perfect confirmation?

Day 4

The Journey Begins

"So Joseph also went up from the town of Nazareth in Galilee to Judea, to Bethlehem the town of David." – Luke 2:4

The journey to Bethlehem was

long, inconvenient, and full of uncertainty. Yet behind the Roman decree that forced Mary and Joseph to travel was divine orchestration fulfilling prophecy. God's guidance often hides within ordinary events.

Years ago, I experienced this kind of subtle direction while traveling through a U.S. airport. As I waited for my flight, I suddenly felt prompted to send a small gift to Paul, a young man in Uganda leading campus fellowships. Within minutes of sending the money, a woman approached me in the crowded terminal and asked, "Are you John Stanko?" She turned out to be from Uganda and began telling me how Paul's ministry had touched her life. I knew then that God had confirmed my decision. The timing was too perfect to be coincidence—it was divine coordination.

Mary and Joseph might have seen only government orders and weary roads, but God saw prophecy unfolding. Likewise, the detours and delays in your life may be God's way of steering you exactly where He wants you to be.

Reflection Questions

Can you recall a moment when God confirmed His guidance through timing or coincidence?

How might your current 'inconvenience' actually be part of His perfect plan?

Day 5

When the Road Is Dark

"The Lord will guide you always; he will satisfy your needs in a sun-scorched land."
– Isaiah 58:11

Nights are longer in December

where I live, but even darkness can become a classroom for trust. God led Israel with a pillar of fire by night—a visible reminder that His light shines brightest in uncertainty. When it's dark to us, it's not for God.

I've often seen this during my overseas ministry trips. Flights have been delayed, bags delayed, plans disrupted—but in those moments, God's direction becomes more vivid. Once in Africa, when an itinerary changed unexpectedly, it caused me to stay longer than I had planned, but it opened the door to ministry connections that lasted for decades. What seemed like disorder and an inconvenience was actually divine redirection. And that has happened to me on many occasions.

Advent teaches that the light does not eliminate darkness—it invades it. God's guidance doesn't mean every detail will be clear, but that His presence will be constant. When your way feels uncertain, remember that His light is not gone; it's simply leading you more closely.

Reflection Questions

When has an unexpected detour in your life turned into divine direction?

How can you remind yourself that God's presence, not clarity, is your true compass?

Day 6

Faith Logic

"We live by faith, not by sight."
– 2 Corinthians 5:7

Faith isn't a leap into the dark as some would have you think—it's a reasoned step into the light. In Acts 16, Paul and his team tried to enter several regions, but the Spirit prevented them.

Then Paul had a vision of a man from Macedonia calling for help. Scripture says, "We *concluded* that God had called us to preach the gospel to them" (emphasis added). They didn't hear an audible voice; they reasoned their way to obedience after a significant albeit symbolic dream.

Faith involves your intellect as much as your emotions. I once studied every New Testament verse related to faith—belief, trust, and unbelief—and discovered that faith is often built on reflection and logic, not impulse. That's why I call it "faith logic." You consider what you know of God's character, your purpose, your gifts, and your past experiences of His faithfulness, then decide to move forward in trust.

The Christmas story reminds us that Joseph, Mary, and the Magi each had to interpret divine direction using both revelation and reasoning. The same Spirit who gives you faith also helps you think.

John W. Stanko

Reflection Questions

How might your reasoning and reflection help you discern God's next step for you?

Are you waiting for a dramatic sign when God has already given you enough light to conclude and act?

Day 7

Get Off Your "But"

"We should go up and take possession of the land, for we can certainly do it."
– Numbers 13:30

When Moses sent spies into Canaan, they returned with a glowing report—then spoiled it with one word: "but." They saw the fruit of God's promise yet fixated on the giants. That single conjunction canceled their courage.

Faith guidance often falters on the word "but." You may say, "I know God is leading me, but I don't have the money… but I'm too old… but I might fail." Those "buts" are not small—they are barriers. Caleb and Joshua saw the same obstacles but framed them differently. Their faith wasn't blind; it was obedient.

Years ago, when I felt called to publish my own books, I had plenty of "buts." No capital. No experience. No safety net. Yet I sensed the Spirit whisper, "Move ahead." When I did, Urban Press was born, and through it, others found their voice too. If I had waited until every "but" was answered, I'd still be waiting, sitting on my "but."

Faith guidance requires silencing the "buts" that keep you from obedience. God rarely calls you when it's convenient—but He always calls you when it's time.

Reflection Questions

What "but" has kept you from moving forward in faith?

How can you replace your "but" with a "because God said"?

Day 8

Faith GPS

"By faith Abraham obeyed and went, even though he did not know where he was going."
– Hebrews 11:8

Abraham followed God without a destination in his travel app. He simply went, trusting that God would guide him one step at a time. His obedience wasn't based on a map, but on a relationship. The same was true for all the characters in the Christmas story.

I call that kind of trust a "faith GPS"—a God Positioning System. In 2014, I left my church position, surrendering most of my income, to start a publishing company. I didn't know where it would lead, but I knew Who had called me. Like Abraham, I walked forward with no guarantees, only promises. Looking back, that step of obedience has sustained me and opened more ministry doors than I could have planned.

Abraham didn't just arrive in faith; he lived in faith. Once he reached the land, he still pitched tents and built altars. God's guidance doesn't end when you arrive—it continues as you abide.

Reflection Questions

How has God's "GPS" led you in seasons when the next step wasn't clear?

What would it look like to follow His direction without demanding full coordinates?

"We'll Be Back" Faith

"We will worship and then we
will come back to you."
– Genesis 22:5

When Abraham climbed Mount Moriah with Isaac, he faced the

greatest test of guidance—obeying a command that made no sense. Yet his faith spoke before the miracle happened: "We'll be back," even though as far as he knew, he was going to sacrifice his son.

Faith guidance sometimes requires acting on what you can't yet explain. Abraham reasoned that if God promised a nation through Isaac, then God could raise Isaac from the dead if necessary. That's faith logic in its purest form—trusting the promise more than the circumstance.

I've had to exercise that kind of faith in ministry many times—when leaving secure positions, launching projects without funding, or helping leaders step into callings that seemed impossible. But every time I obeyed, God provided exactly what was needed. Faith that speaks "we'll be back" honors God even before the outcome appears.

This Advent, let your faith speak life into the unknown. Say with confidence, "I don't know how, but I know Who."

Reflection Questions

Where do you need to declare "we'll be back" faith today?

How can your words reflect the trust you already hold in your heart?

Day 9

FaithSpeak

"The Lord who rescued me from the paw of the lion and the paw of the bear will rescue me from the hand of this Philistine."
– 1 Samuel 17:37

    Before David ever faced Goliath, he had already spoken victory. His words were not arrogance—they were in alignment with God's track record. Faith guidance begins when your mouth agrees with what your spirit already knows.

I've seen this in my own journey. Many times, I've said aloud what I believed God was about to do—long before it happened. I once told a group, "We're going to build a network of leaders who live by purpose all over the world." At the time, I had a handful of contacts and no budget. Yet within years, that faith declaration became reality through PurposeQuest International and continues this day in Pakistan, Kenya, Uganda, Colombia, and the United States.

Faith doesn't deny obstacles; it declares outcomes. David didn't say, "I hope God will help." He said, "He will." When your words reflect trust, your steps follow as Goliath discovered to his demise.

Reflection Questions

What declaration of faith can you speak today that aligns with God's past faithfulness?

How can you use your words to reinforce rather than weaken your trust in His guidance?

Day 10

Put Me In, Coach

"Then I heard the voice of the Lord saying, 'Whom shall I send? And who will go for us?' And I said, 'Here am I. Send me!'"
– Isaiah 6:8

Isaiah's response to God's question is the essence of guidance: availability.

Many wait for perfect conditions before saying yes, but divine direction begins with willingness, not readiness.

I remember sitting at breakfast with a friend who told me, "You need to write something for us older folks—something about not retiring from purpose." That conversation birthed my book *Never Too Old for Purpose*. I realized I wasn't finished; God was calling me to keep serving, teaching, and creating well into my seventies. I could almost hear myself praying one of my favorite prayers, "Put me in, Coach!" That is my slogan to help me live a bold life.

Like Isaiah, you don't have to understand the full assignment to respond to the call. You simply have to say yes. God provides the details as you move. This Advent season, as we celebrate the One who said yes to leave heaven for earth, may we echo that same spirit of obedience.

Reflection Questions

Where might God be asking you to step up rather than step back?

How can you make yourself more available to His call today?

Day 11

Touched by Your Work

"God did extraordinary miracles through Paul, so that even handkerchiefs and aprons that had touched him were taken to the sick, and their illnesses were cured and the evil spirits

left them."
– Acts 19:11-12

When God guides you, He can use even your ordinary work to touch lives in extraordinary ways. Paul's handkerchiefs and aprons were simple tools of his trade, yet God used them as vessels of healing.

I often tell leaders that their purpose impact extends far beyond what they see. Years ago, I began posting weekly devotionals and purpose lessons online. Later, while traveling abroad, someone approached me and said, "Your writing changed my life." I didn't even know they were reading! Like Paul's aprons, my words had traveled farther than I could imagine.

Never underestimate how God can multiply your obedience. The work of your hands may reach places your feet never will. Let Him use your skills, creativity, and faithfulness as conduits of grace.

Reflection Questions

How might God use your ordinary work to accomplish extraordinary results?

Who could be "touched" by something you've created, written, or shared?

Your Spiritual Shadow

"As a result, people brought the sick into the streets and laid them on beds and mats so that at least Peter's shadow might fall on some of them as he passed by." – Acts 5:15

Peter's shadow didn't heal people—God did. But his nearness to God's presence was so real that even proximity to him brought change and blessing. Your "shadow"—your influence—can also carry divine impact.

I think about the leaders, writers, and pastors I've mentored who are now guiding others across the world. Some I taught decades ago; others I've never met in person. Yet God uses what I've deposited to continue shaping lives long after our conversations end. Like Peter, I'm reminded that we don't have to strive to be influential; we simply walk in step with the Spirit, and our shadow does the rest.

You may not see the full fruit of your obedience now, but God multiplies it through unseen influence. Stay faithful to your purpose, even when the results are invisible.

Reflection Questions

Who might be walking in the light of your "spiritual shadow"?

How can you intentionally cultivate a presence that points others to Christ?

Purpose Glory

"In the same way, let your light shine before others, that they may see your good deeds and glorify your Father in heaven."
– Matthew 5:16

Sometimes God's guidance becomes visible to us through divine connections. I've had people come up to me in airports, at churches, in malls, on vacations, and even in countries like Cuba, South Africa, Kenya and England to ask if I was John Stanko. They all knew me, or knew of my work and they wanted to share how what I had said or wrote had helped them in a time when they seeking God's will for some part of their life. That's what Christmas reminds us of—how God's light came into the world through one life, and now shines through ours wherever we go.

Guidance often unfolds this way—not through burning bushes, but through glimpses of fruit you didn't even know you'd sown. Each story, book, and trip has become a light God uses to glorify Himself. Jesus said our light should shine not for our fame but for His. When others see God's hand in your work, it's a reminder that you're walking in step with divine purpose.

Reflection Questions

What unexpected encounters have reminded you that God is guiding your steps?

How can you reflect glory back to Him through your daily work and service?

Never Too Old to Serve

"Now give me this hill country that the Lord promised me that day." – Joshua 14:12

Caleb was eighty-five when he asked for more territory. He didn't say,

"I've done enough," but instead said in so many words, "Put me in, Coach." I relate to that. At seventy-five as I celebrate this Christmas, I'm still writing, coaching, and traveling, believing God isn't finished using me.

In *Never Too Old for Purpose,* I wrote that old age is not an excuse but an opportunity. Like Simeon and Anna, your latter years can be your most fruitful if you stay sensitive to the Spirit. Purpose doesn't expire—it evolves. God's guidance doesn't stop when your job does; it continues as long as your heart beats.

Advent reminds us that both young and old played roles in the Christmas story—Mary and Joseph, Simeon and Anna, shepherds and wise men. Age only limits you if your thinking does.

Reflection Questions

What "hill country" is God still asking you to claim in this season of life?

How can you encourage others to see age as an asset for God's Kingdom?

Day 15

Provision on the Journey

"And my God will meet all your needs according to the riches of his glory in Christ Jesus."
– Philippians 4:19

Paul wrote these words while in

prison, not enjoying prosperity. His secret? He had learned to be content in every financial season. I've lived in those seasons myself—times of abundance and times of lack—but each one revealed God's faithfulness.

In *Purpose Full Provision*, I wrote that God sometimes allows "financial famine" to test what's in your heart and to remind you He's your source. More than once, I've seen God provide through unexpected channels: surprise donations, publishing opportunities, or friends or just acquaintances who felt prompted to help. Those moments weren't just about money—they were about trust.

If you're walking through a lean season this Advent, don't despair. The same God who sent manna in the wilderness still provides daily bread for those who seek Him—and do His will.

Reflection Questions

How has God met your needs in unexpected ways?

What financial fears do you need to replace with faith this Christmas?

Faith to Innovate

"Isaac planted crops in that land and the same year reaped a hundredfold, because the Lord blessed him."
– Genesis 26:12

When the famine struck, Isaac stayed where God told him. Instead of fleeing to Egypt, he innovated—he dug new wells. In obedience, he found abundance.

I've learned that innovation often emerges from crisis. During ministry transitions or times of scarcity, God has shown me new ways to serve—developing online courses, expanding publishing, or creating global mentorship networks. What began as necessity became creativity.

Isaac's "faith to innovate" mirrors God's guidance today. When the world retreats, believers advance. Advent celebrates the same truth: God sent new light into old darkness. Guidance doesn't just help you survive—it helps you invent.

Reflection Questions

Where might God be inviting you to innovate rather than escape?

How can you see your limitations as invitations to creativity?

Day 17

Waiting for Guidance

"Now there was a man in Jerusalem called Simeon... It had been revealed to him by the Holy Spirit that he would not die before he had seen the Lord's Messiah." – Luke 2:25–26

Simeon spent a lifetime waiting for the fulfillment of a promise. There's no record of how long he waited, only that he was faithful in the meantime. Waiting is not wasted time when God is your guide—it's preparation.

I've learned that lesson repeatedly. When I felt prompted to write *Never Too Old for Purpose*, I sensed the urgency of the message but not the timing. I waited for months, then years, while God refined both my perspective and the audience He wanted to reach. When the time came, the words flowed effortlessly. What felt like delay was actually divine alignment.

God's timing rarely matches ours, but His purpose never fails. Advent teaches us that even the longest waits end in fulfillment. Simeon and Anna remind us that those who stay ready never miss their moment of revelation—or purpose.

Reflection Questions

How might God be using your waiting season to prepare you for something new?

What helps you stay faithful while you wait for His direction?

Divine Detours

"A man's heart plans his way, but
the Lord directs his steps."
– Proverbs 16:9

    Sometimes God's guidance looks like disruption. Detours are not denials—they're redirections. I've experienced this often in ministry and travel.

Once, my passport was stolen in an African country, on my way to the airport to depart no less. My unexpected prolonged stay, while painful, opened many doors for future ministry work. God knew what He was doing; I now like to think that the thief was God's agent who was doing His will without realizing it!

Joseph and Mary's journey to Bethlehem was also a divine detour. What seemed like a government inconvenience was actually God fulfilling prophecy. When God reroutes your plans, He's not punishing you; He's positioning you.

We tend to measure faithfulness by consistency, but God measures it by responsiveness. Trust the interruptions. They may be heaven's way of leading you exactly where you need to be.

Reflection Questions

Can you recall a time when an unexpected change led to unexpected blessing?

How can you stay flexible and trust God when your plans are disrupted?

When God Changes Your Plans

"Many are the plans in a person's heart, but it is the Lord's purpose that prevails." – Proverbs 19:21

    I once thought my career path was set in stone—pastoring, teaching, writing. Then God changed the plan. He led me to start a publishing company, a move that didn't fit my comfort zone or my schedule. Yet that redirection became the platform for Urban Press and an entire generation of purpose-centered authors.

Mary and Joseph faced their own plan changes—an unexpected pregnancy, a last-minute trip, a stable instead of an inn, a relocation to Egypt. Yet every change carried them closer to God's plan and purpose. When God redirects you, it's never random; it's redemptive.

Guidance requires the courage to release your version of the plan so that God's better one can unfold. What feels like loss of control is actually the gain of divine purpose.

Reflection Questions

Where might God be inviting you to release control so He can redirect your steps?

What new opportunity could be hidden inside your change of plans?

Day 20

Purpose in the Pause

"Be still, and know that I am God." – Psalm 46:10

There's purpose in every pause. We live in a world that glorifies movement, but God often guides us through stillness. Between major seasons of ministry, I've learned that waiting is a divine classroom. It's where God redefines success, renews priorities, and restores strength.

Before Isaiah's great commission—"Here am I, send me"—he spent time in God's presence, seeing His holiness and confessing his weakness. Before the disciples preached, they waited in Jerusalem. Pauses aren't punishment; they're preparation. I spent 11 years as an associate pastor, during which I spoke from the pulpit two times—the second time was on the last Sunday I was at the church. I was waiting and learning, but now I am going, while still learning.

In *Put Me In, Coach*, I wrote that God calls prepared players, not spectators. Stillness is part of that training. When we resist the urge to rush ahead, we give God space to shape our hearts before He reveals the next step.

Reflection Questions

What "pause" might God be using right now to prepare you for greater impact?

How can you turn waiting into worship instead of frustration?

Day 21

Guided to Give

"You will be enriched in every way so that you can be generous on every occasion."
– 2 Corinthians 9:11

God's guidance often leads us to generosity. In *Purpose Full Provision*, I wrote that divine supply is never meant to stop with us; it flows through us. I've seen that repeatedly—whether giving to a child's education in Kenya or providing books for a rural library, every act of giving opened doors for greater ministry and blessing.

The wise men followed divine guidance to Jesus, and their first response was giving. Their gifts weren't just treasures; they were expressions of worship. When you give according to God's leading, your generosity becomes an extension of His mission.

Ask God where He wants you to invest this Christmas. The guidance you seek might come through the generosity you show.

Reflection Questions

How might generosity become a form of guidance in your life?

What step of giving could God be prompting you to take this season?

Day 22

Peace as a Compass

"Let the peace of Christ
rule in your hearts."
– Colossians 3:15

Peace is one of the most reliable indicators of God's guidance. It's not the absence of conflict but the presence of clarity. In *Unlocking the Power of Your Thinking*, I wrote that when your thoughts align with truth, peace follows—and that peace becomes your compass.

When I've had to make difficult decisions—leaving positions, starting new ventures, or turning down opportunities—the deciding factor was often inner peace. When I forced something, anxiety grew; when I followed peace, provision followed.

Mary's story shows this beautifully. She pondered, questioned, and finally embraced peace in God's will. Let peace—not pressure—be your guide this Advent.

Reflection Questions

How can you better recognize when peace is leading and when fear is pushing?

What situation in your life needs the calm rule of Christ's peace today?

Day 23

From Promise to Fulfillment

"Blessed is she who has believed that the Lord would fulfill his promises to her!" – Luke 1:45

Faith doesn't end with a promise—it endures until fulfillment. Both

Elizabeth and Mary carried promises that seemed impossible. Yet in God's time, they were fulfilled.

I've seen that pattern in my own journey. Projects that took years to develop—books, ministries, partnerships—eventually blossomed beyond anything I imagined. Looking back, I see that every delay, every closed door, was part of God's choreography.

Guidance often feels incomplete until hindsight reveals how perfectly it fit together. As you approach Christmas, remember that the promise God gave you is not forgotten—it's simply unfolding.

Reflection Questions

What promise are you still believing God to fulfill?

How can you nurture faith and patience while you wait for His timing?

Day 24

Guided by Obedience

"When he saw them, he said, 'Go, show yourselves to the priests.' And as they went, they were cleansed."
– Luke 17:14

Ten lepers cried out for mercy, but Jesus didn't heal them immediately. Instead, He gave them a command: "Go." Healing came as they went.

That principle has marked my own journey. When God instructed me to launch new initiatives—PurposeQuest, Urban Press, leadership academies, youth centers—I often saw no immediate results. But every time I obeyed, blessing followed movement. Divine guidance usually begins with obedience, not confirmation.

Faith doesn't wait for the finish line to appear before running. It starts at the sound of God's voice. The lepers' cleansing wasn't dependent on perfect understanding; it was dependent on perfect trust. The same will be true for you this Christmas season.

Reflection Questions

What step of obedience might God be asking you to take before you see the result?

How can you strengthen your "as you go" faith this week?

Day 25

Guided Through Correction

"Then neither do I condemn you," Jesus declared. "Go now and leave your life of sin." – John 8:11

Guidance isn't only about direction; it's also about correction. Jesus offered both to the woman caught in adultery. His grace forgave her, and His truth guided her forward.

In *Go and Obey*, I wrote that when God corrects, He doesn't humiliate—He reorients. Many of us remember moments when the Holy Spirit convicted us, not to shame us but to guide us toward freedom. I've had my share of course corrections, times when I had to admit that my motives or methods needed adjusting. Yet every correction cleared the path for fresh purpose.

God's redirection is one of the greatest gifts of His guidance. If you sense conviction today, don't resist it—receive it. Correction means He still has a plan for you.

Reflection Questions

How has God used correction to bring new direction in your life?

What area might the Spirit be inviting you to release or realign?

Day 26

Guided by Purpose Early

"Speak, Lord,
for your servant is listening."
– 1 Samuel 3:10

Samuel was a boy when he first heard God's voice. His story reminds us that divine guidance doesn't wait for adulthood—it begins with openness regardless of age.

In *Never Too Young for Purpose*, I shared how I've seen children and teens around the world hear from God, serve in ministry, and discover their calling early in life. During my work in Colombia, I watched students lead worship, teach peers, and even interpret for adults. They didn't see their age as a limitation but as a stage for obedience.

Purpose has no age restriction. Whether young or old, the key is the same: a listening heart. This Christmas, let Samuel's prayer be yours—"Speak, Lord, I'm listening."

Reflection Questions

How can you encourage younger generations to recognize God's voice?

What helps you keep a childlike heart that listens for His guidance?

Guided by Faith in the Dark

"He told him, '
Go, wash in the Pool of Siloam.'
So the man went and washed,
and came home seeing."
– John 9:7

The blind man didn't receive sight until he obeyed Jesus' command to go wash. Imagine walking through crowded streets blind, heading to a pool you can't see, based only on a word you heard. That's faith-guided obedience.

I've lived this principle often—taking steps that didn't make logical sense but felt divinely right. Whether launching a new ministry, traveling to a new country, or funding a project before resources appeared, God honored obedience rooted in trust.

Faith doesn't always remove uncertainty; it transforms it into opportunity. If you're facing a "go and wash" moment, remember: the miracle happens when you're in motion.

Reflection Questions

Where might God be asking you to obey before understanding?

How can you strengthen your faith to act even when you can't see?

Day 28

Guided to the Manger

"When they saw the star, they were overjoyed."
– Matthew 2:10

The wise men's journey began with a star and ended with worship.

Their story is the perfect picture of divine guidance—God leading hearts hungry for truth to the feet of Jesus.

I've experienced this same kind of guidance in ministry: divine connections, chance encounters, and open doors that could only be explained by God's hand. Like the Magi, I've discovered that true guidance always leads to worship. Every success, every journey, every "yes" points back to Him.

As you celebrate Christmas, follow the same light that led them. It won't just show you a destination—it will lead you into adoration.

Reflection Questions

What "star" has God placed in your life to draw you closer to Jesus?

How can you let your life's journey lead others to worship Him?

Day 29

Guided to Serve

"Go and make preparations for
us to eat the Passover."
– Luke 22:8

Before Jesus shared His final meal with His disciples, He gave them a simple task: "Go and prepare." Their obedience in a small assignment became part of the greatest story ever told.

Service is one of the clearest forms of divine guidance. God rarely calls us to do glamorous things, but He often invites us to serve faithfully behind the scenes. I've learned that every major ministry breakthrough in my life began with small acts of obedience—helping, teaching, giving, preparing.

In serving, we find direction; in humility, we discover purpose. Guidance begins not when we lead but when we serve.

Reflection Questions

What act of service might God be using to guide your next step?

How can you cultivate a heart that sees serving as sacred?

Guided to Cast Again

"Go to the lake
and throw out your line."
– Matthew 17:27

When Peter was facing a financial problem, Jesus didn't hand him a coin—He sent him fishing. The miracle came through obedience to a familiar skill used in a new way.

I've had many "cast again" moments. When a project failed or a plan stalled, God often said, "Try again." Years ago, I wanted to stop writing after a series of disappointments, but God kept urging me to cast the net one more time. That act of persistence birthed new books and ministries that have blessed others far beyond what I imagined.

Guidance often means returning to what you know, but this time with renewed faith. The same lake, the same net—but a fresh word from God makes all the difference.

Reflection Questions

Where might God be asking you to "cast again"?

How can you approach familiar tasks with renewed faith and expectation?

Day 31

Guided to Influence the Young

"We will tell the next generation
the praiseworthy deeds of
the Lord, his power,
and the wonders he has done."
– Psalm 78:4

When God guides you, His plan almost always includes someone younger. His purposes move forward as one generation invests in the next.

In *Never Too Young for Purpose*, I shared how I've seen God ignite vision in children and youth across the world—from the schools of Colombia to the youth centers in Africa. Those young people weren't waiting to grow up before serving; they were already leading, praying, and dreaming with God. Guidance doesn't skip generations—it multiplies through them.

Each time I visit one of our PurposeQuest libraries or meet with students who've read one of my books, I'm reminded that influence is stewardship. Our example, encouragement, and faith become the tools God uses to guide others. If you want to see where His light is leading next, then find a way to invest in the next generation.

Reflection Questions

Who among the younger generation could benefit from your mentorship or encouragement?

How can you invest your time, wisdom, or resources to help them discover their purpose?

Day 32

Guided to Encourage Others

"Let us consider how we may spur one another on toward love and good deeds." – Hebrews 10:24

Sometimes God's guidance takes the form of a nudge to speak life into someone else. Encouragement is not just kindness—it's a divine strategy.

I've often watched how one timely word can change the trajectory of a person's faith. Whether through my *Monday Memos*, coaching sessions, or overseas teaching, I've learned that encouragement releases courage. People don't need us to fix everything; they need us to remind them of what God has already placed within them.

Jesus constantly encouraged His followers. He told Peter, "I have prayed for you that your faith may not fail." Even knowing Peter's weakness, Jesus affirmed his divine purpose. When we do the same—seeing others not for who they are now but for who they're becoming—we participate in God's guidance for their lives.

Reflection Questions

Who needs a word of encouragement from you this week?

How can you make encouragement a consistent part of your ministry and relationships?

Day 33

Guided by the Spirit's Voice

"Whether you turn to the right
or to the left, your ears will hear
a voice behind you, saying,
'This is the way; walk in it.'"
– Isaiah 30:21

God's Spirit is not silent; He is constantly guiding those who listen. The challenge is rarely that He isn't speaking—it's that our lives are too noisy to hear.

I've experienced moments when a still, inner prompting led me to call someone at just the right time or give in a way I hadn't planned. Those nudges became divine appointments. In *Unlocking the Power of Your Faith*, I wrote that hearing from God isn't reserved for the spiritually elite—it's the birthright of every believer who learns to listen, believing He has something to say.

The Spirit's guidance is gentle but sure. As you end the year, take time to quiet your heart. God often whispers next steps between moments of worship and rest. His voice won't compete with your distractions, but it will always confirm His peace.

Reflection Questions

What helps you discern the difference between God's voice and your own thoughts?

How can you make space to listen for His guidance each day?

Guided Into A New Year

"The Lord will guide you always;
he will satisfy your needs in
a sun-scorched land and will
strengthen your frame."
– Isaiah 58:11

Every new year invites us to trust God afresh. Guidance isn't just for the past year's challenges—it's for the new roads ahead.

Looking back, I see that every chapter of my life—teaching, writing, traveling, leading—was guided by God's steady hand. None of it was random; all of it was preparation for the next stage. From *Purpose Full Provision* to *Go and Obey*, one truth stands firm: when you follow God's light, He never leads you into darkness.

As we step into a new year, let's do so with confidence. The same God who guided shepherds by starlight and prophets by vision is still guiding you by His Spirit. The path may not be clear, but His presence is certain. And your best purpose days are just around the corner.

Reflection Questions

What have you learned about God's guidance this year that you can carry into the next?

How can you enter the new year with faith, gratitude, and expectation?

Conclusion

Guided Still

As this devotional journey draws to a close, I hope you see that God's guidance is not reserved for special moments or holy seasons—it's the rhythm of daily life with Him. From the first "yes" of Mary to the faith of the shepherds, the Christmas story reminds us that divine direction always begins with trust and obedience. The same God who guided wise men by starlight continues to lead you by His Spirit's light.

Throughout these pages, you've read of guidance that comes through waiting, serving, giving, listening, and sometimes starting over. That same pattern will continue long after Advent ends. God's light never dims; it simply moves with you into every new chapter.

So as you move forward, keep your lamp trimmed and burning. Listen for His whisper in both the ordinary and the extraordinary. And remember: wherever He leads, His presence goes before you, making even the darkest paths bright with purpose and peace.

How To Follow John W. Stanko

The Monday Memo

Every Sunday since 2001 I have written a *Monday Memo* to discuss topics like purpose, creativity, and faith. You can access it at:
www.purposequest.com

The Stanko Bible Study

I have completed a verse-by-verse commentary on the New Testament and I am not writing a weekly entry in the Purpose Study Bible that examines the topics of purpose, creativity, goal setting, time management, and faith as they are found in the Old Testament. All these studies for both the Old and New Testaments can be found at www.purposequest.com

All My Books

Are available for purchase on Amazon or through the Urban Press website http://www.urbanpress.us

My Free Mobile App

You can download the PurposeQuest app from https://subsplash.com/purposequestinternationa/app
I have many hours of video and audio teaching there.

My Website

http://www.purposequest.com has all my video and audio teachings, plus some print material, Monday Memo, weekly Bible lesson, and the daily devotional.

Social Media

I publish daily material on all my social media outlets: Facebook, Instagram, Twitter, LinkedIn, TikTok, and YouTube. You can easily find and follow me on any of those outlets by using my first and last name.

And of course, I am always available through my email address:
johnstanko@gmail.com

Additional Titles by John W. Stanko

A Daily Dose of Proverbs
A Daily Taste of Proverbs
Changing the Way We Do Church
I Wrote This Book on Purpose
Life Is A Gold Mine: Can You Dig It?
Strictly Business
The Faith Files, Volume 1
The Faith Files, Volume 2
The Faith Files, Volume 3
The Leadership Walk
The Price of Leadership
Unlocking the Power of Your Creativity
Unlocking the Power of Your Productivity
Unlocking the Power of Your Purpose
Unlocking the Power of You
What Would Jesus Ask You Today?
Your Life Matters
Live the Word Commentary: Matthew
Live the Word Commentary: Mark
Live the Word Commentary: Luke
Live the Word Commentary: John
Live the Word Commentary: Acts
Live the Word Commentary: Romans
Live the Word Commentary: 1 & 2 Corinthians
Live the Word Commentary: Galatians, Ephesians, Philippians, Colossians, Philemon
Live the Word Commentary: 1 & 2 Thessalonians, 1 & 2 Timothy, and Titus
Live the Word Commentary: Hebrews
Live the Word Commentary: Revelation

Ediciones en Español

Cambiando la Manera de Hacer Iglesia

La Vida Es Una Mina De Oro: ¿Te Atreves A Cavarla?

No Leas Estes Libro: (A Menos Que Quieras Convertirte E Un Mejor Lider)

Fuero lo Viejo, Adentro lo Nuevo

Gemas de Propósito

Ven a Adorarlo: Preparándonos para Emmanuel

Desbloqueando el Poder de Tu Pensamiento

Nunca Demasiado Joven para un Propósito

Nunca Demasiado Viejo Para Un Propósito

Estrictamente Negocios

Biblia de Estudio del Propósito: Deuteronomio

Biblia de Estudio del Propósito: Josué

Entrenamiento para Reinar

Puntos De Poder

El Poder del Púrpura

Póngame, Entrenador

Avivamiento del Propósito

Made in the USA
Middletown, DE
08 December 2025